THE GREEKS

Mark McArthur-Christie

Series editor **Sue Palmer**

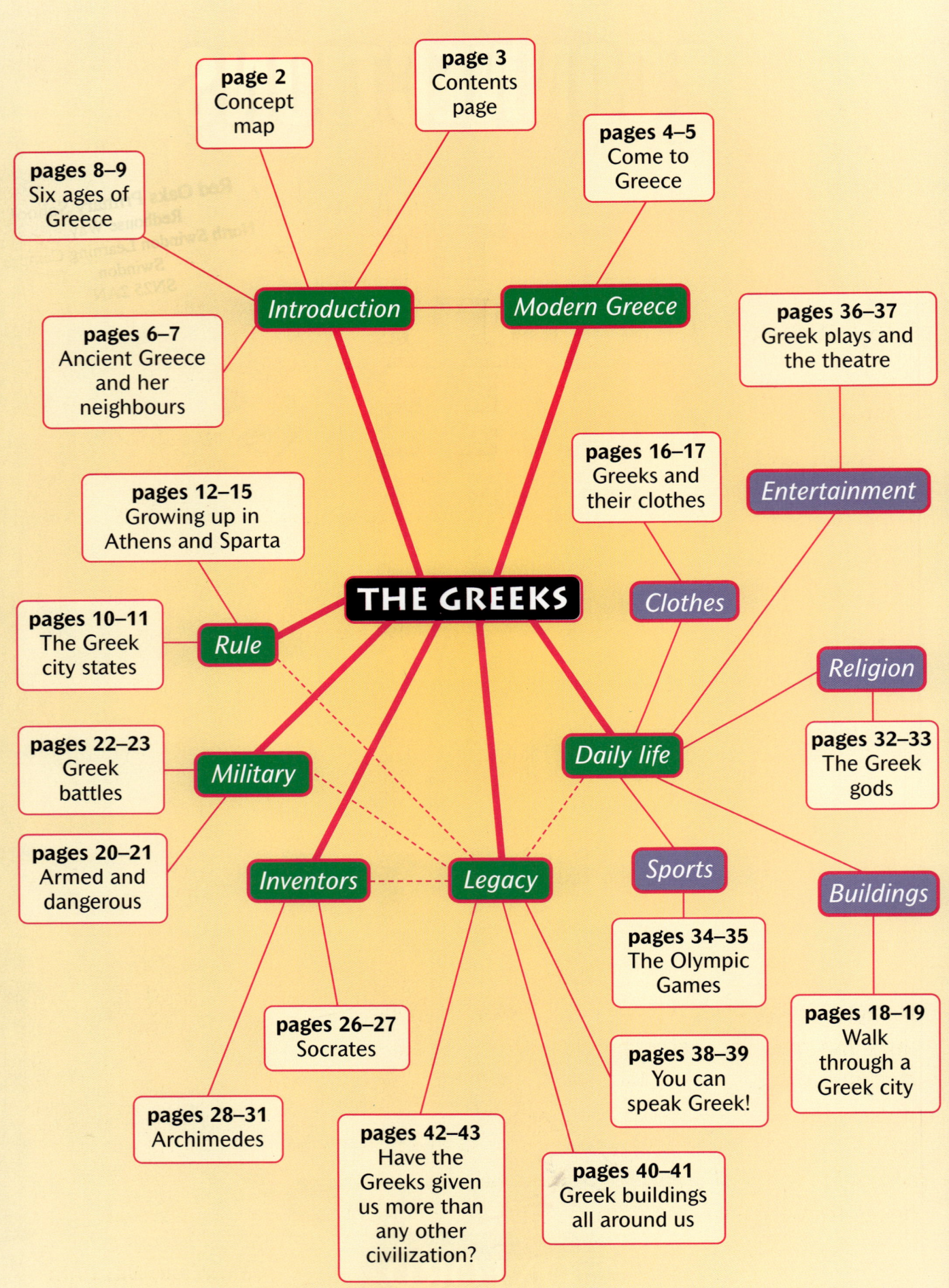

CONTENTS

Come to Greece! 4
Ancient Greece and her neighbours 6
The six ages of Greece 8
The Greek city states 10
Growing up in Athens and Sparta 12
Greeks and their clothes 16
Walk through a Greek city 18
Armed and dangerous – lethal Greeks 20
Greek battles 22
Socrates 26
Archimedes 28

Eureka 30
The Greek gods 32
The Olympic Games 34
Greek plays and the theatre 36
You can speak Greek! 38
Greek buildings all around us 40
Have the Greeks given us more than any other civilization? 42
Glossary 44
Bibliography 45
Index 46

Ancient Greek societies were very different from ours, but many of their achievements made our civilization possible. My favourite part of this book is the story of Archimedes and the way in which he devised a method of testing the purity of a gold crown. "Eureka!" he cried when he discovered the answer to the problem.

Professor Michael Vickers
Ashmolean Museum

COME TO GREECE!

VISIT THE PLACE WHERE WESTERN CIVILIZATION BEGAN…

Greece is amazing! Everywhere you look, the past is all around – it's like walking through history. You can go into temple courtyards and touch pillars, stones and sculptures that are 25 centuries old. You can see tiny carved jewels, no bigger than your thumbnail, that were made 400 years BC – that's more than 30 lifetimes ago!

Temple of Apollo Bassae

PEACEFUL COUNTRYSIDE…

Amid breathtaking scenery and charming villages there are many spectacular ruins to see. The temple of Apollo Bassae, dedicated to the god Apollo, is hidden away miles from any town in beautiful rural Arcadia. Some historians think this temple was designed by the same **architect** who built the Parthenon on the **Acropolis**, which towers above bustling Athens. The Parthenon is still there today in this exciting capital city – so why not visit it?

…OR BIG CITY

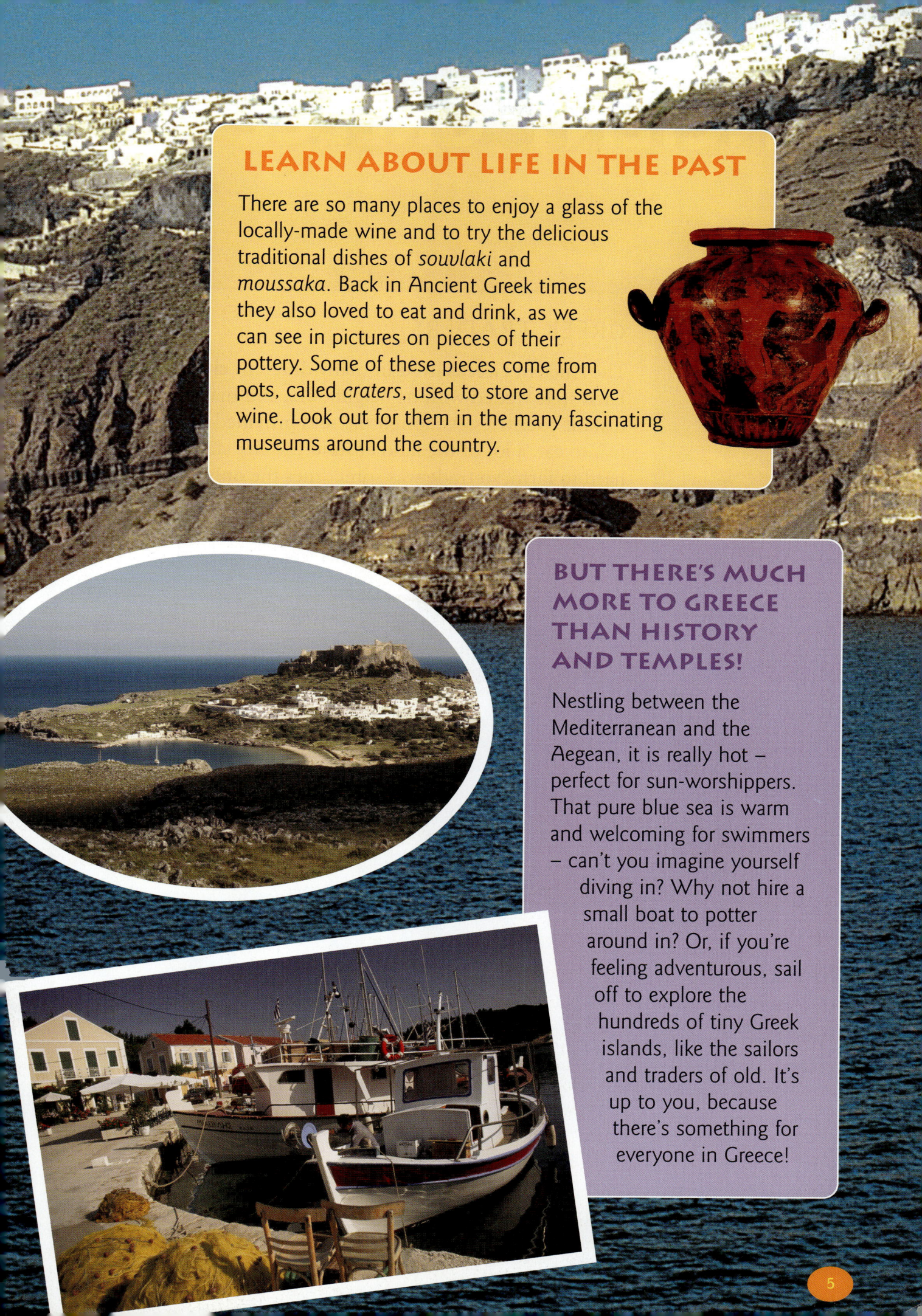

LEARN ABOUT LIFE IN THE PAST

There are so many places to enjoy a glass of the locally-made wine and to try the delicious traditional dishes of *souvlaki* and *moussaka*. Back in Ancient Greek times they also loved to eat and drink, as we can see in pictures on pieces of their pottery. Some of these pieces come from pots, called *craters*, used to store and serve wine. Look out for them in the many fascinating museums around the country.

BUT THERE'S MUCH MORE TO GREECE THAN HISTORY AND TEMPLES!

Nestling between the Mediterranean and the Aegean, it is really hot – perfect for sun-worshippers. That pure blue sea is warm and welcoming for swimmers – can't you imagine yourself diving in? Why not hire a small boat to potter around in? Or, if you're feeling adventurous, sail off to explore the hundreds of tiny Greek islands, like the sailors and traders of old. It's up to you, because there's something for everyone in Greece!

ANCIENT GREECE AND

GREEK TRADERS

The Ancient Greeks lived in many different **city states**. Each state traded with its neighbours, and many distant countries. Although the seas provided plenty of fish to eat, a lot of the land around the city states was hard to farm, so trade was sometimes the only way the city states could make money to buy food. The land around the Mediterranean was rich in minerals and precious metals which the Greeks traded for food.

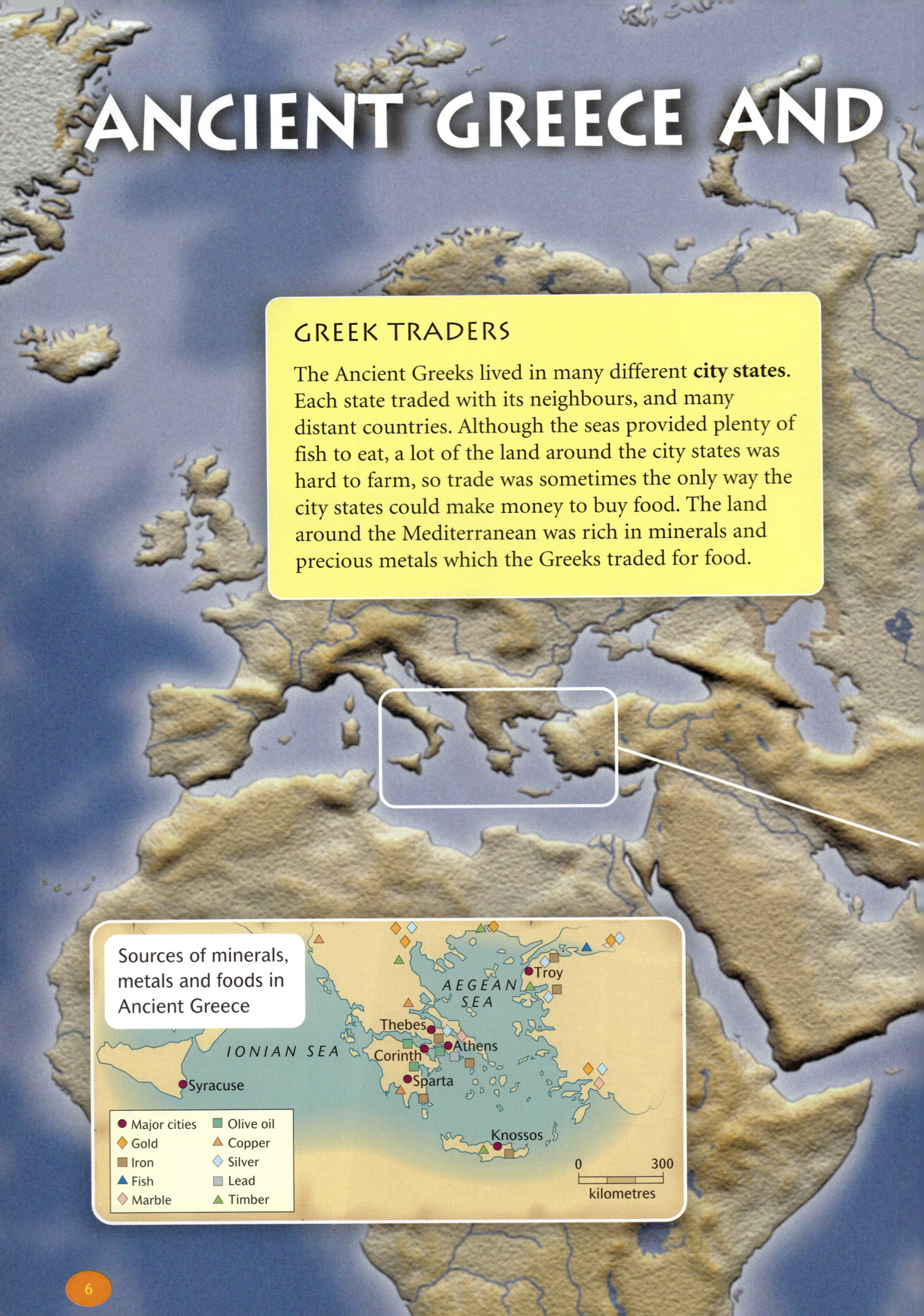

Sources of minerals, metals and foods in Ancient Greece

- Major cities
- Gold
- Iron
- Fish
- Marble
- Olive oil
- Copper
- Silver
- Lead
- Timber

HER NEIGHBOURS

WARS AND ALLIANCES

Sometimes people think of Ancient Greece as a peaceful place where people simply spent their days talking in the agora, going to parties and the theatre, inventing things or trading with others. In fact, Greece was far from stable and peaceful. Throughout its history there were wars between Greek city states and wars with other countries. Some city states formed alliances with each other – joining together to fight another city state. The two most powerful **alliances** were the Athenian League and the Spartan Alliance who fought each other regularly. You can see from the map below which city states were in the Athenian League and which were in the Spartan Alliance.

THE SIX AGES OF GREECE

THE BRONZE AGE
c.3,000 BC–1,100 BC

c.2,000–1,700 BC
Myceneans conquer mainland Greece

c.1,200 BC
The Trojan War

427 BC
Plato born – pupil of Socrates and teacher of Aristotle

c.460–429 BC
Pericles becomes leader of Athens and makes the city great

c.469 BC
Socrates born

490 BC
Battle of Marathon

CLASSICAL PERIOD
500–400 BC

431–404 BC
The Peloponnesian Wars – war between Athens and Sparta

448 BC
Peace with the Persians

480 BC
Persians defeated at the sea battle of Salamis

c. 500 BC
The first triremes sail

404 BC
Athens surrenders to Sparta

395–340 BC
War between groups of rival city states

336–323 BC
Alexander the Great's reign begins – ruler of all Ancient Greece and beyond

LATE CLASSICAL PERIOD
400–330 BC

338–336 BC
Macedonian king, Phillip 11, unites the Greek city states into a body known as the Council of Corinthian League

323–148 BC
After the death of Alexander the Great w resume between riva groups of city states

c. 1,100 BC
End of Mycenean civilization.
Early Greek **city states** ruled by kings

THE DARK AGE
1,100–800 BC

c. 800–700 BC
The kings begin to be replaced by aristocratic republics

c. 600–500 BC
Coin currency introduced

c. 625 BC
Birth of Thales – the first known **philosopher**

776 BC
The first Olympic Games

ARCHAIC PERIOD
900 BC–500 BC

507 BC
Democracy in Athens was begun by Cleisthenes

c. 750–700 BC
Invention of the Greek alphabet

296–79 BC
First Roman victories over Greek cities

146 BC
Corinth destroyed by the Romans

HELLENISTIC PERIOD
330–300 BC

c. 287 BC
Archimedes born

167 BC
Macedonia, north of Greece, conquered by the Romans

86 BC
Athens is invaded and raided by the Romans

THE GREEK CITY STATES

'LIKE FROGS ROUND A POND'

Plato said that Greek **city states** were 'like frogs round a pond'. This is because they were positioned around the Aegean Sea – some on the mainland, some on islands – and were separated by natural boundaries, such as mountains or the sea. These boundaries made communication difficult, so the city states developed very differently and often went to war with each other.

Despite their differences, however, the Greeks were united about one thing: the Greek language. They believed it made them different from and better than everyone else. In fact, they claimed that non-Greeks made a sound like 'bar-bar-bar' when they spoke – so they nicknamed them 'barbarians'.

WHO IS IN CHARGE?

Just as the city states fought each other, so different political ideas were fought over within the city states. Each was ruled in a different way. People talked about different sorts of government and argued over which was best, so Greek city states often changed the person who was in charge and the way the state was run. Among the different methods were:

- monarchy – when a king or queen rules
- oligarchy – when a few people rule
- timocracy – rule by the rich
- aristocracy – rule by people born into 'ruling class'
- tyranny – the strongest person rules
- democracy – adult male citizens rule by casting a vote.

TWO CITY STATES

SPARTA

- Landlocked, inward-looking, nervous
- The city is more important than the individual
- Discipline, a hard life and simplicity are best
- All males from ages 7-30 serve in the army all year round
- Trade forbidden
- Strict laws made by the kings

GOVERNMENT

Ephorate (5 men)
Kings (2)
Aristocratic Council (28 nobles)
All Spartan men

ATHENS

- Near the sea, outward-looking, adventurous
- The individual is more important than the city state
- Intelligence, thought and ideas are best
- No full-time army
- Trade with other city states and countries
- Laws decided by citizens' votes

GOVERNMENT

Assembly (all Athenian men)
Council (500 Athenian men, drawn by lot)

GROWING UP IN ATHENS

Education was one way the **city state** made sure that its citizens knew what was important and how they were supposed to behave. Athenian and Spartan schools were very different, but they did have a few things in common: discipline was harsh, pupils were often beaten, and schools were only for boys. Girls stayed at home and learned **domestic** skills. When they grew up they were not allowed to own property, vote or have important public jobs other than as **priestesses**.

GROWING UP THE HARD WAY IN SPARTA

The Spartans educated their boys to be stronger, braver and tougher than each other, as well as neighbouring rivals. The schools were really barracks where everyone was a soldier – even from the age of seven. Although educated at home, the women in Sparta were also brought up to be tough and taught to fight.

When a boy started at a Spartan school he was given no clothes or shoes, just a cloak. He was also given horrible food to eat – and not much of it, which forced some of the boys to steal more food. This was intended to make the boys tougher so they could fight harder, and become cunning and resourceful so they would win in battle.

The boys worked together as an *agela*, meaning *'herd'*. They slept on wooden pallets in barracks and pulled up reeds from the river bank to spread on top of the hard pallets to make their beds.

THE SPARTAN BOY AND THE FOX

There is a legend that one Spartan boy was so hungry he caught a fox and hid it under his cloak to eat later. He had to stand on parade with the other boys for so long that the fox started gnawing into his stomach. The boy knew he would be in trouble if he cried out, so he had to force himself to stay still and not make a sound. This legend was meant to show how tough Spartan soldiers were. Some historians think it was **propaganda** invented by the Spartans to scare their enemies.

AND SPARTA

AGE 7–17
- All boys lived together in barracks

AGE 18–19
- Start of military and athletic training

AGE 20–29
- Young soldiers begin fighting in the Spartan army
- Soldiers could get married, but still lived in barracks with the other soldiers

AGE 30–60
- Soldiers became equals – a full member of Spartan society
- Soldiers could live at home, but were still part of the army

AGE 60+
- Soldiers could now retire and, if they were **elected**, become a member of the government

GROWING UP THE CIVILIZED WAY IN ATHENS

Growing up in Athens, boys were educated to be **civilized** and to become fit and agile. Until they were old enough to go to school, boys were taught at home by a special slave called a *paedagogus*. Being a paedagogus was not easy – if a pupil gave the wrong answers or misbehaved, it was the paedagogus that would be beaten not the pupil.

THE GYMNASIUM

When they were five, boys went to their local school, known as the **gymnasium**. They usually stayed there until they were fourteen, unless their parents were rich, in which case they then might stay until eighteen. In the classroom, the boys sat on hard benches and they learned by listening to the teacher as he read or recited. The boys would write what they heard on **wax tablets** using a **stylus**, and then memorize what they had written. Anyone who was unable to remember the lesson would be given a beating.

As well as reading, writing and mathematics, the boys learned poetry and music: everyone had to be able to play the **lyre**. Athenians thought that poor lyre-playing was a sign that someone was badly brought up and uncivilized. Another important subject was physical education – every gymnasium had space for running and athletics.

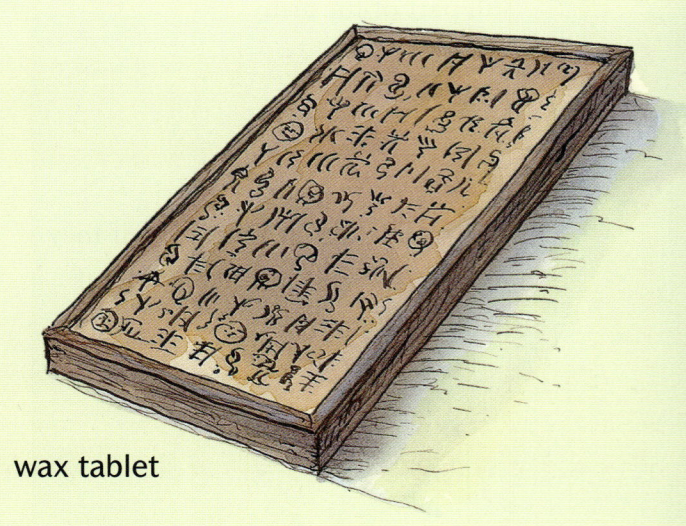

wax tablet

WHO TAUGHT WHAT?

Paidotribes
Physical fitness and gymnastics

Kitharistes
Poetry and music

Grammatistes
Reading, writing and basic mathematics

THE ACADEMY

After the gymnasium, students went on to the Academy, which was like a university. Subjects like philosophy (how to think), ethics (the study of right and wrong); and rhetoric (how to make speeches) were taught. Most large city states had an Academy, and the largest was in Athens. Only the students from rich families could afford to go to the Academy – many boys had to start work straight after school to earn a living.

GREEKS AND THEIR CLOTHES

BEAUTIFUL BODIES

The Greeks thought that the human body was a beautiful thing. Many paintings on pieces of pottery, as well as sculptures of the body, have been discovered in the ruins of ancient cities and temples. How their bodies looked was very important to the Greeks, so they spent a lot of time exercising and playing sports. They usually did this naked! The word '**gymnasium**', where boys were taught sports, comes from the Greek word *gumnos*, meaning naked.

The Greeks also believed that clothes should show off their bodies. Their neighbours in other countries wore trousers and clothes with sleeves, but the Greeks preferred more elegant clothing, with carefully arranged drapes and pleats. Often they were not very practical, particularly as they did not wear any underwear.

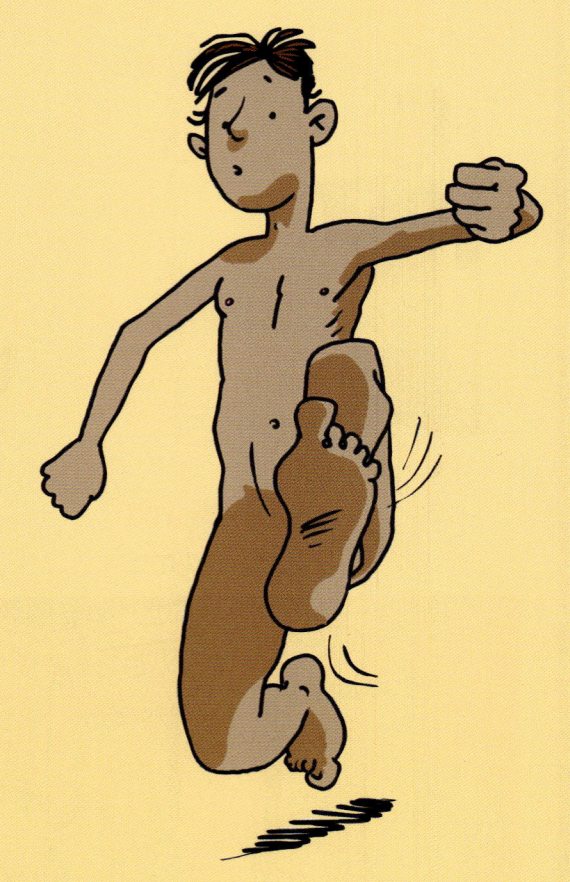

EVERYDAY CLOTHES

When the weather was cold, a long woollen garment called a *peplos* was worn. It draped around the body so that it hung in tight folds, showing off the wearer's shape. In warmer weather, most Greek men and women wore linen *chitons* (pronounced ky-ton). The *chiton* was made from a large cloth rectangle, held with pins at the shoulders and tied at the waist. Old men and women wore long *chitons*, and young men wore shorter ones.

TRAVELLING CLOTHES

When they were travelling, Greeks often wore a *petasos* – a hat with a wide brim, and a strap to keep it on if the wind blew. A *himation* could be draped over the *chiton* for warmth, which was made from a similar rectangle of cloth, usually made from wool.

Although many *chitons* were probably plain white linen, the Greeks loved colour and they often dyed cloth. Sometimes they even dyed the wool while it was still on the sheep!

Make your own Chiton

What you need

- A rectangle of cloth, 2 m long and 1 m wide, sewn in half
- Needle and thread
- Belt
- 2 safety pins

1
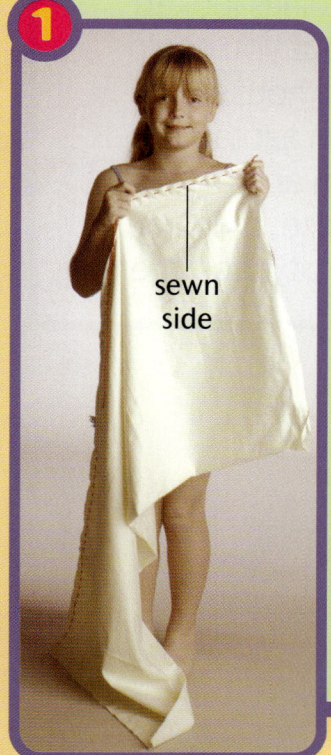
sewn side

2

3

pin   pin

4
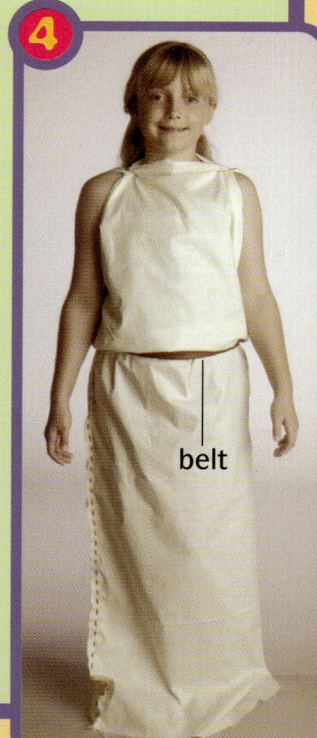
belt

17

WALK THROUGH A

HOMES

The rooms of Greek homes were built around a central courtyard. The most important room was the *andron*, or dining room, where only men would attend *symposiums* (drinking parties). Other rooms included the women's quarters, bedrooms, storerooms, kitchen and, in some houses, a very basic toilet and drains.

Houses were usually made from materials from the local area, perhaps stone or locally-made brick. Their floors were often decorated with **mosaics** made of pebbles, but a few grand houses even had carpets.

The Greeks had very fixed ideas about the buildings in their cities. Each **city state's** buildings looked different, but you could always find houses, temples, an agora, gymnasium and theatres. Without these, the Greeks believed a city was inferior.

TEMPLES

- Places where Greeks could honour their gods
- Outside altar for worship (a statue of the god would be inside)
- Animals sacrificed to the gods
- Statues specially sculpted to make temples grand and important
- Temples usually painted in bright colours. See examples on pages 4–5 and pages 40–41

GREEK CITY

THE AGORA

- The heart of the city
- Council meetings held here in a council chamber
- Traders bought and sold here
- People met to talk or do business
- Sometimes special entertainments for the crowds – actors and comedians
- *Stoas* (parades of shops and meeting places) around the edge

THE GYMNASIUM

- Every city had one – see page 14
- Physical education very important – central space for running and athletics
- Small classrooms built around the open space

THE THEATRE

- Theatres usually on a slope
- Plays performed in the open, with painted scenery as background
- Hard wooden or stone seats (people brought cushions)
- Seats in semi-circle
- Sound had to carry a long way; theatres specially designed so audience could hear actors. See pages 36–37

19

ARMED AND DANGEROUS

GREEK ARMOUR AND WEAPONS

The Greeks were often at war, both on land and at sea, so they became good at making **arms** and **armour**. Because the Greeks fought mostly in groups that did not move around much, they could afford to wear heavy, protective armour. Unfortunately for the Greek soldier, he had to pay for all his equipment himself! Take a look at this *hoplite* (a type of Greek soldier) and see how he would have defended himself and attacked his enemies.

Helmet
- Corinthian helmet
- heavy

Spear
- lethal
- 2 m long
- needle sharp

Sword
- straight bladed
- **falacatas** had curved blades

Armour
- protects body in battle
- bronze armour – expensive
- leather armour – cheaper (covered with bronze sheeting)

Leg guards
- protect legs in battle
- bronze
- tough

– LETHAL GREEKS

TRIREMES

The Greeks' best fighting ship was the trireme, so called because it had three tiers of oars. It was powered by 170 rowers, sitting on benches on the ship's three decks. Designed to be fast and lethal, it was built to ram and sink enemy ships. The *trireme* was also a mobile platform for the spearmen and archers who lined its decks, ready to pelt the enemy with spears and arrows.

TRIREME

KEY DATA
LENGTH 40 metres
HEIGHT 3 metres
WIDTH 6 metres
TOP SPEED 14 knots
CREW 14 spearmen, 4 archers, 25 officers crew, 170 rowers
KEY BATTLE VICTORY Salamis, 480BC against Persia
KEY STRENGTHS speed, manoeuvrability.
BATTLE TACTIC diekplous (break through and ram)

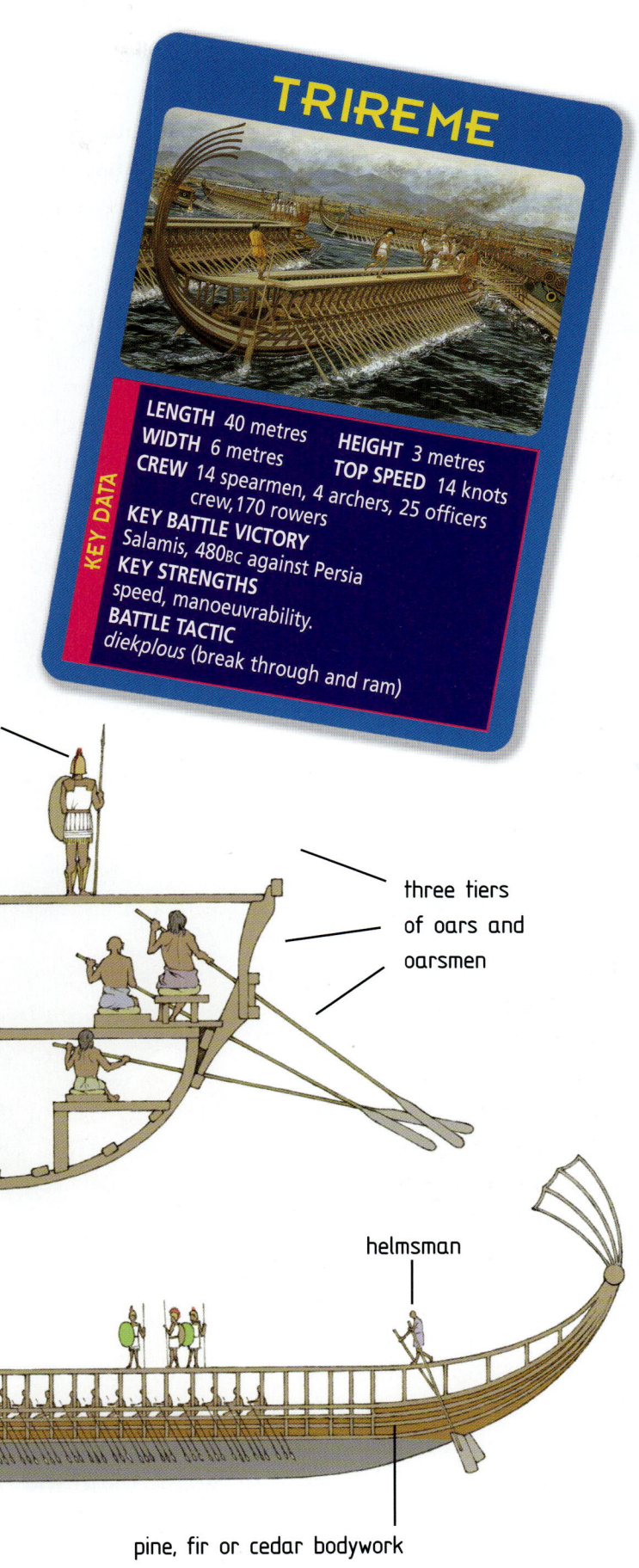

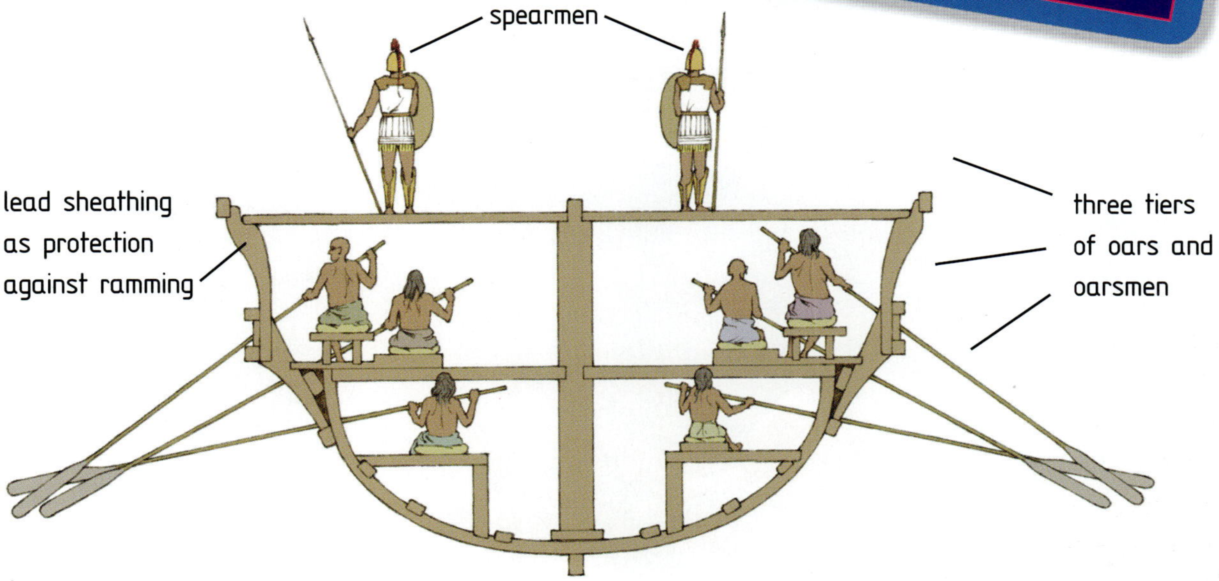

spearmen

lead sheathing as protection against ramming

three tiers of oars and oarsmen

archers

helmsman

bronze sheeting for strength when ramming

pine, fir or cedar bodywork

GREEK BATTLES

The Greeks loved to talk and write about their history, particularly their **military exploits**. They liked **myths** as well, usually about their gods and goddesses but sometimes stories about past battles such as the **legend** of the Trojan Horse.

THE STORY OF THE TROJAN HORSE

The Greeks had **besieged** the city of Troy in an attempt to rescue Helen, the wife of King Menelaus. She had been kidnapped by Paris, the Prince of Troy, and was also considered the most beautiful woman in the world. After ten years of fighting the Greeks were unable to break through the city's high wall, so they needed a new **strategy**. They built a giant, hollow wooden horse and filled it with soldiers.

Meanwhile, the rest of the Greeks went back to their ships and sailed away from Troy, which fooled the Trojans into thinking that the Greeks had given up and had left the horse as a gift. During the party the Trojans held to celebrate the 'victory', the Greeks sneaked out of the horse and opened the gates of Troy to their comrades, who had sailed back under the cover of darkness. By daylight, the Greeks had taken the whole city and won the battle.

As well as the many battles known through myths and legends, there were written accounts of actual battles, such as those between the Athenians and Spartans, and between the Greeks and the Persians. The Battle of Salamis and the Battle of Marathon are amongst the most well known.

XERXES SMASHED AT SALAMIS

Xerxes' navy surrounded

SALAMIS, 480 BC

PERSIAN KING XERXES WATCHED HIS FLEET SMASHED BY THE GREEK NAVY TODAY in a decisive sea-battle just off the coast of Attica. Themistocles, the Athenian admiral, commented, "The Persians had seven hundred ships and we had just three hundred, but our smarter tactics beat the barbarians."

Themistocles went on to explain how his choice of the narrow strait between Salamis and Attica meant the Persians' bigger fleet was forced into defeat. The Persians could only get three ships at a time into the strait, and by the time they had all sailed in, the Greek navy was ready to strike.

Using his faster, better-crewed triremes, Themistocles surrounded Xerxes' navy with a circular 'wooden wall' of fighting ships. There was no escape for the Persians, who lost two hundred ships.

Commentators now think that Xerxes will have to rethink his plans for an invasion of Greece. The Persian leader was unavailable for comment.

> IT'S AN EARLY BATH FOR THE PERSIANS

Xerxes, Persian leader

MARATHON MASSACRE

We were grossly outnumbered – just my men and a thousand brave Plataens who arrived just in time. There weren't even enough troops to form a proper battleline. I put my best men on the **flanks** and the weaker troops in the centre and advanced across the plain of Marathon towards the enemy. When the battle began the weaker men gave way but the flanks circled around, attacked from behind, and forced the Persians to retreat. It was a tough decision but it paid off – we won!

General Miltiades, Athenian commander

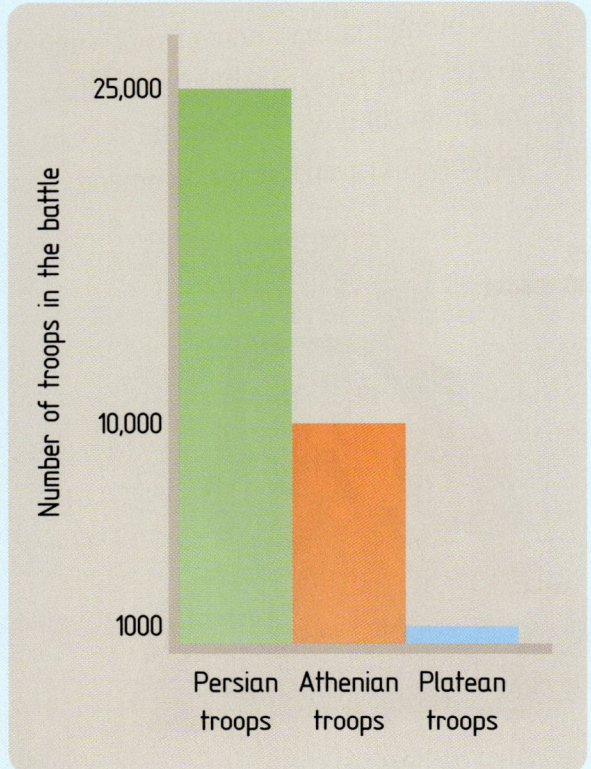

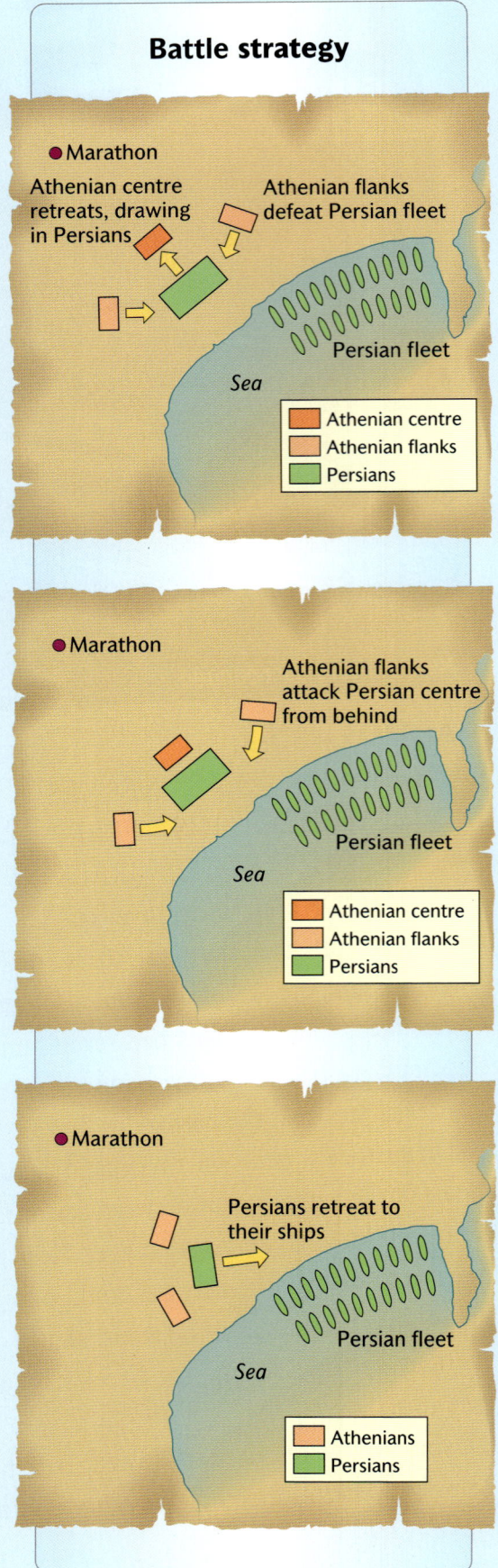

Battle strategy

- Marathon
Athenian centre retreats, drawing in Persians
Athenian flanks defeat Persian fleet
Persian fleet
Sea
Athenian centre
Athenian flanks
Persians

- Marathon
Athenian flanks attack Persian centre from behind
Persian fleet
Sea
Athenian centre
Athenian flanks
Persians

- Marathon
Persians retreat to their ships
Persian fleet
Sea
Athenians
Persians

FOR MILTIADES

Persian troops arrive in Greece

Athenian troops arrive near where Persians landed

Philippides sent to get help from Spartans

Philippides returns – Spartans can not come yet (religious festival)

Battle!

Victory for the Greeks.

MYTHICAL ENDING

As the story of this battle was retold and written down, people added a more dramatic ending. They said that Philippides ran the long distance from Marathon to Athens to give news of the victory. Unfortunately, he did so with his dying breath.

SOCRATES

Socrates was a great thinker who lived in the fifth century BC. Other Greek **philosophers** were interested in how the world was made, but Socrates was more interested in thoughts and ideas. His pursuit of truth through the questioning of established ideas made him one of the most famous philosophers of all time, but it also led to his death.

Socrates was born in Athens, some time between 471 and 469 BC. Like most Athenian boys, he went to school and learned about mathematics and philosophy as well as sport and gymnastics. After school he worked for a while as a sculptor, and also served as a soldier in the Athenian army. He was a brave fighter and saved the lives of many comrades.

Socrates believed the gods wanted him to be a teacher, so when he left the army he began teaching philosophy – the science of how to think. He did this by asking his students questions about subjects such as 'justice', 'knowledge' and 'happiness' to make them think clearly and logically about what these words meant. This technique has become known as 'the Socratic method' and we know about it because one of his students, called Plato, wrote down accounts of many of these philosophical conversations. They show just how clever Socrates was in showing up people who did not think clearly.

Plato's writings show Socrates to be a great teacher – kind, humorous and modest, but with a marvellous grasp of logic and human nature. He was also very popular with his students, and was often seen in public places in Athens, surrounded by them, discussing ideas and politics.

It was this that led to his downfall. A powerful group of Athenian leaders did not like the way he questioned the way things were and they felt threatened by Socrates and his ideas. In 399 BC they accused him of corrupting the young people of Athens and put him on trial. At his trial Socrates made a famous speech, which was written down by Plato. His enemies prevailed, however, and Socrates was condemned to death. According to the Greek custom, he was given a cup of poison to drink, called hemlock. He sat with his friends around him and drank it as though it were a goblet of wine, then waited serenely for his death.

'The Death of Socrates' painted by Jacques-Louis David in 1787

ARCHIMEDES
A PICTURE TIMELINE

c.287 BC
- Archimedes born in Syracuse, a Greek city in Sicily

264-241 BC
- Eureka! See pages 30-31

- Archimedes invents the lever and the pulley
- 1st **Punic Wars** against the Romans begins

280 BC   270 BC   260 BC   250 BC

270-264 BC
- Archimedes studies mathematics with **Euclid's** followers in Alexandria, Egypt
- Invents the Archimedes Screw for raising water

218–212 BC

- Archimedes begins inventing military weapons to defend Syracuse against the Romans

- The Burning Mirror

- The Claw for lowering Greek military ships into the water quickly or **capsizing** enemy ships

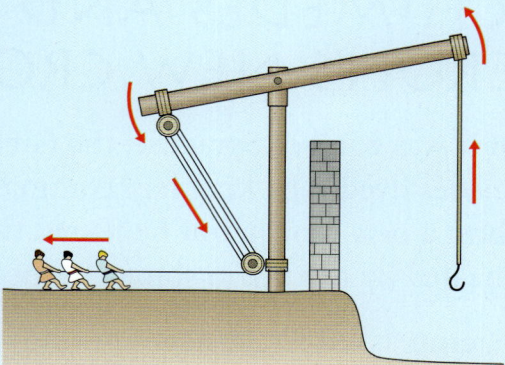

- The Catapult

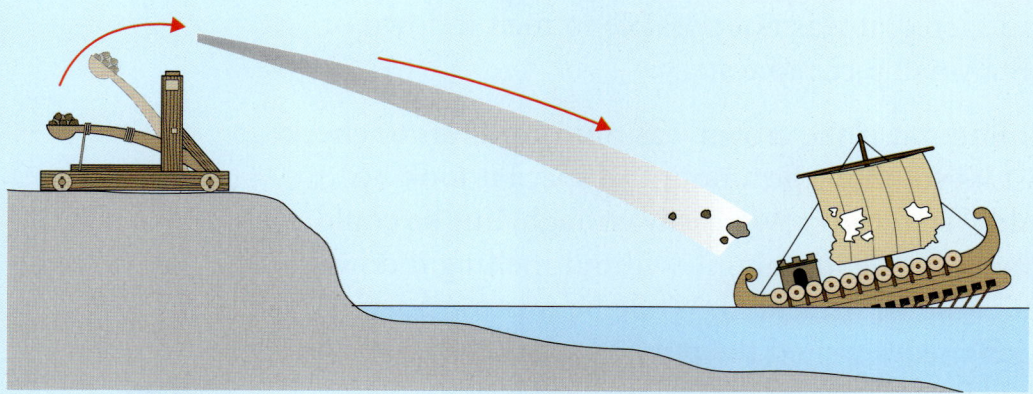

- 2nd **Punic Wars** begins

240 BC   230 BC   220 BC   210 BC

212 BC
- Romans invade Syracuse
- Death of Archimedes

EUREKA!

Archimedes noticed that when an object is put into a liquid, it makes the level of the liquid rise by the same volume as that of the object. There is a **legend** about this scientific discovery.

ARCHIMEDES AND KING HIERON'S NEW CROWN

Hieron II was King of Syracuse, the Greek city where Archimedes lived. The king had commanded a goldsmith to make him a new crown, but he feared the goldsmith might have cheated by mixing in some cheaper materials.

King Hieron asked Archimedes to find a way to check that the crown was made completely of gold. However, because it was very valuable and sacred, it was not possible to melt it down or even to break off a small piece to test.

The only way to find out if the crown was pure gold was to check its weight against its volume (the amount of space it took up). Archimedes could weigh the crown easily enough, but he could not think of a way to judge its volume without melting it down into a shape that could be measured. While he was considering this problem, Archimedes visited the public baths and, as he climbed in, he noticed that the water level went up. "Eureka!" he cried (meaning "I have discovered it!"). He was so pleased with his solution that he is said to have run home naked, still calling out "Eureka!"

Archimedes had noticed that, when an object is placed in water, it displaces some of that water. He worked out that the volume of water displaced must be equal to the volume of the object. Therefore, he could put the crown into a tank of water and measure the volume of water it displaced. He could then put a lump of pure gold (the same weight as the crown) into the same tank. If it displaced exactly the same amount of water, the crown must also be pure gold.

A LEVER LONG ENOUGH TO MOVE THE WORLD

Archimedes invented the lever to be able to lift heavy objects.

We still use levers like those used by Archimedes. Modern engineers divide them into three groups or 'classes'. Here are three types of lever and how we use them today.

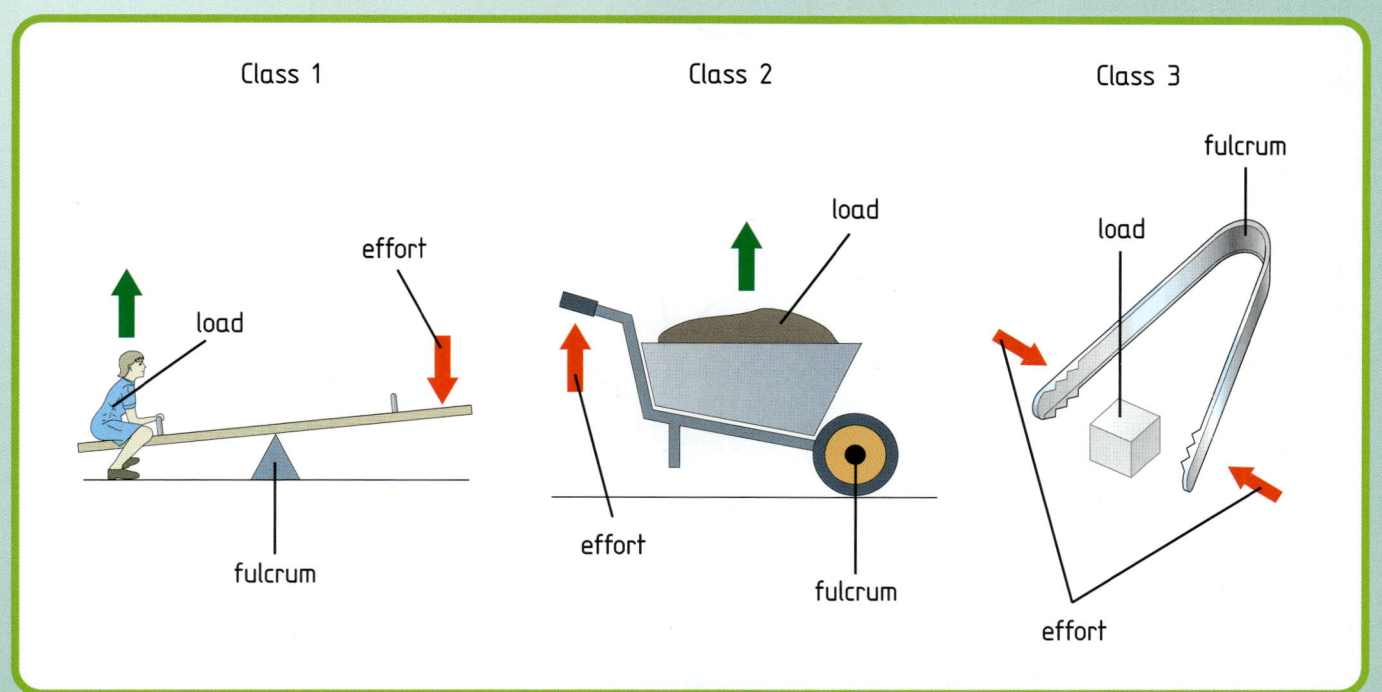

THE GREEK GODS

The Greeks did not believe in just one god. They believed in many gods and goddesses all representing a different aspect of life. These gods were believed to live on Olympus, the highest mountain in Greece, but in the stories that were told they often interfered in the daily lives of their worshippers.

The Greeks believed that the gods were not always kind and good and often caused problems. This helped the Greeks explain why things went wrong in the world around them. The stories they made up about the gods and goddesses were a little like modern soap operas.

The Greeks worshipped their gods and heroes by making sacrifices to them. The worshippers would gather together to kill an animal and burn the fat and bones on a special stone table called an altar. They believed that the gods enjoyed the smell of the burning fat and bones while the Greeks ate the cooked meat themselves. The special days when the sacrifices were held were days off for everyone. This made religion very popular and everyone joined in.

As well as the gods, the Greeks also believed that some men were half man and half god, called heroes. They had superhuman strength and were almost as powerful as the gods. The most well known is Hercules.

THE OLYMPIC GAMES

All Greek boys were trained from an early age to be athletes. Athletics and sports were very important to the Greeks. They thought physical ability was part of *arete* – a Greek word that means excellence. All Greek boys wanted to compete one day in the Olympic Games because it was the most important contest in the Greek empire. It was so important that the Greeks stopped fighting each other and declared a **truce**.

The games were held every four years as part of a special religious festival honouring Zeus. During the Games, the Greeks made a grand sacrifice to Zeus, called a *hecatomb*; it involved sacrificing one hundred head of cattle in the god's honour.

WHAT WERE THE EVENTS OF THE ANCIENT OLYMPICS?

BOXING
Boxing was hard. Fighters could hit their opponent when he had fallen down, and there were no 'rounds' to give the boxers a rest.

WRESTLING
Greek wrestlers had to be tough because they could have their fingers broken, be kicked in the stomach or even be killed!

PANKRATION
Pankration was a combination of boxing without gloves and wrestling. It was very violent. Contestants could kick their opponent in the stomach or break his bones to win!

RUNNING
Greek athletes were great runners. They ran short sprints as well as medium distance races. One race was even run in full **armour**, which would have weighed more than 25 kg.

CHARIOT RACING

There were two sorts of chariot race, one with four horses and another with just two. Racing chariots were very light so they could go as fast as possible.

HORSE RACING

Greek jockeys rode without stirrups for more than 5 km, so had to be excellent riders!

PENTATHLON

The Pentathlon was a long and difficult event involving five activities. Athletes had to throw a discus and a javelin as well as run, jump and wrestle.

GREEK PLAYS AND

The Ancient Greek plays started out as events during the festivals of particular gods. These were often all-day events in which many plays were staged and the audience usually ate and drank throughout the performances. Nevertheless, the plays themselves were not just for entertainment – they often had a serious moral or political point.

Greek plays were performed in open-air theatres, in daylight. This meant that the theatres had no roofs and were open to the hot Greek sun as well as the rain. At first, they were built from wood set into hillsides, so that all the audience had a view of the stage. Later theatres were built from stone.

Greek theatres were often very big – some could hold as many as 20,000 people – and some had secret passages allowing 'special effects' to be staged. For instance, actors playing ghosts could suddenly appear on stage.

Lines were sung or chanted. They were spoken not just by the few actors performing but also by a group of people called the *chorus*. The performers in the *chorus* usually stood at the side of the stage as they chanted: they were like a **narrator**.

The Greeks believed that the words in a play were the most important thing, but as the theatres grew they also had elaborate costumes and masks. This was so that the members of the audience sitting furthest away from the stage could still see the performers and know which character was speaking.

THE THEATRE

There were moral plays, with themes such as greed and pride. These were called tragedies, because they had sad and gory endings. However, the Greeks loved comedies too, and these often poked fun at politicians or famous people.

WHO WROTE THE PLAYS?

AESCHYLUS (525–456 BC)
- Famous for tragedies
- Wrote *The Persians* (about the Battle of Salamis)
- Acted, trained the chorus and wrote songs

SOPHOCLES (496–406 BC)
- Wrote more than 100 plays
- Wrote *Antigone* and *King Oedipus*

ARISTOPHANES (460/450–c.386 BC)
- Wrote comedies
- Most famous plays are *The Birds*, *The Wasps* and *The Frogs*

EURIPIDES (485–406 BC)
- Called 'father of **melodrama**'
- Wrote *The Trojan Women* and *Medea*

YOU CAN SPEAK GREEK!

You may not have realized it, but you can speak Ancient Greek! Modern English has its roots in the Greek language spoken more than two thousand years ago. Even our word for the letters we use is Greek – *alphabet*. Try breaking it down and you get 'alpha' and 'bet'. The first two letters of the ancient Greek alphabet were 'alpha' and 'beta'.

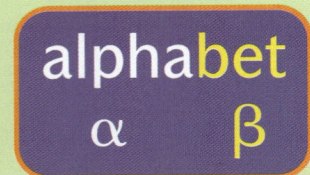

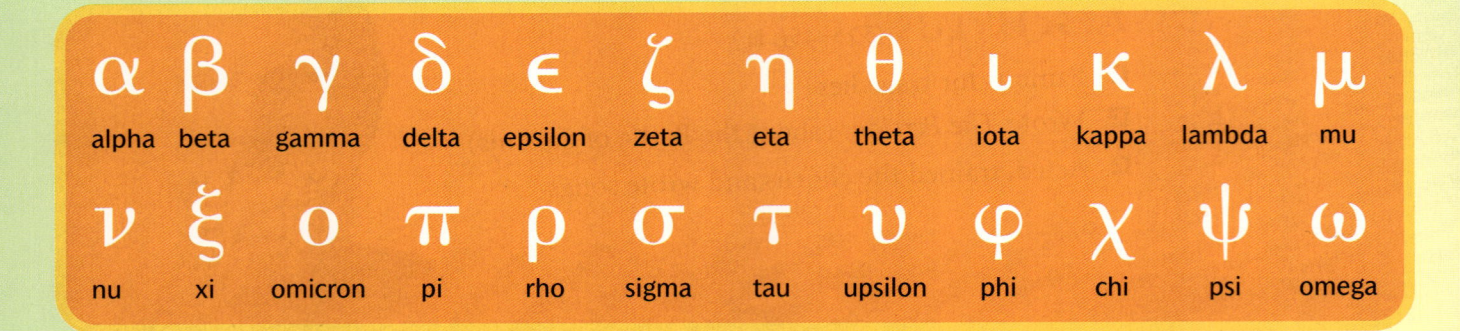

alphabet
α β

α	β	γ	δ	ε	ζ	η	θ	ι	κ	λ	μ
alpha	beta	gamma	delta	epsilon	zeta	eta	theta	iota	kappa	lambda	mu
ν	ξ	ο	π	ρ	σ	τ	υ	φ	χ	ψ	ω
nu	xi	omicron	pi	rho	sigma	tau	upsilon	phi	chi	psi	omega

BE A GREEK DETECTIVE

Ancient Greek words have sneaked into our language over hundreds of years. We can hardly notice they are there now, unless we do some detective work…

There are bits of Ancient Greek words hidden in lots of modern words that we use every day. If you know what the Greek word means you can often work out what the whole word means.

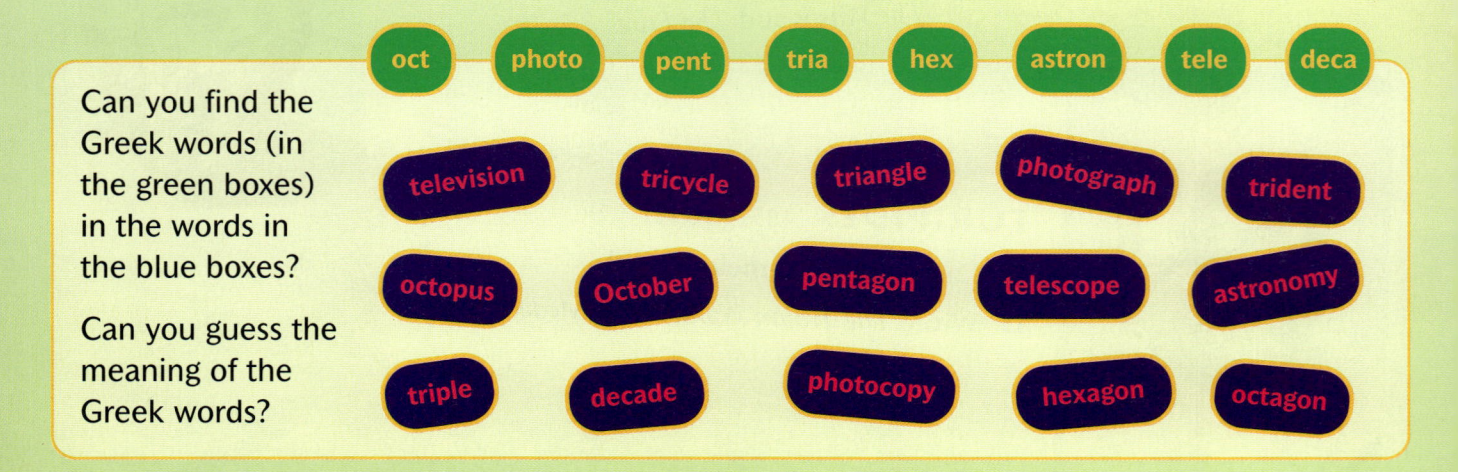

oct — photo — pent — tria — hex — astron — tele — deca

Can you find the Greek words (in the green boxes) in the words in the blue boxes?

Can you guess the meaning of the Greek words?

television, tricycle, triangle, photograph, trident, octopus, October, pentagon, telescope, astronomy, triple, decade, photocopy, hexagon, octagon

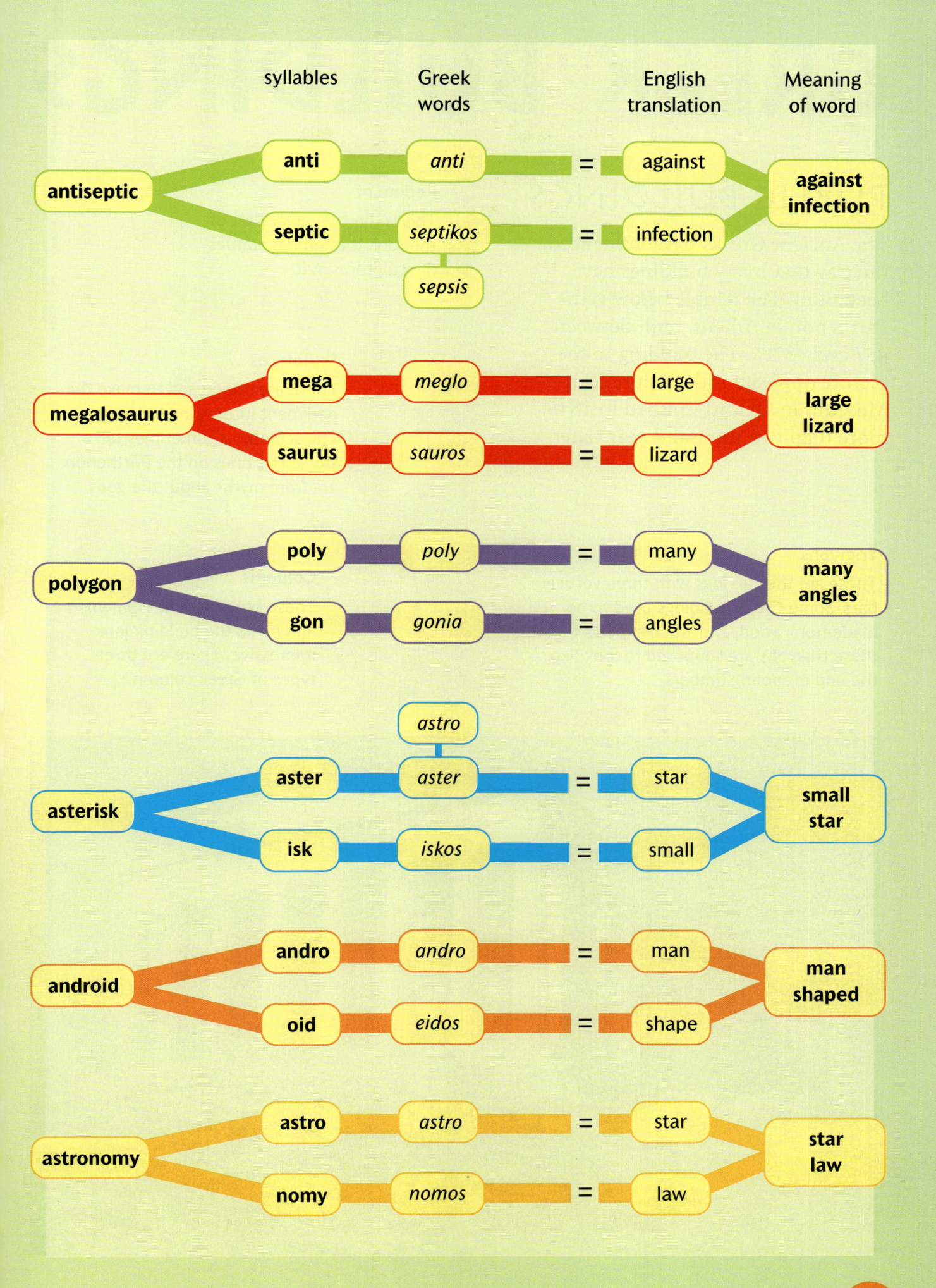

	syllables	Greek words		English translation	Meaning of word
antiseptic	**anti**	*anti*	=	against	against infection
	septic	*septikos*	=	infection	
		sepsis			
megalosaurus	**mega**	*meglo*	=	large	large lizard
	saurus	*sauros*	=	lizard	
polygon	**poly**	*poly*	=	many	many angles
	gon	*gonia*	=	angles	
asterisk		*astro*			
	aster	*aster*	=	star	small star
	isk	*iskos*	=	small	
android	**andro**	*andro*	=	man	man shaped
	oid	*eidos*	=	shape	
astronomy	**astro**	*astro*	=	star	star law
	nomy	*nomos*	=	law	

GREEK BUILDINGS

PUBLIC BUILDINGS

The Ancient Greeks have influenced the way that many buildings have been built. The temple below is the Parthenon in Athens, built between 437 and 432 BC. The building in the picture opposite is the Ashmolean Museum in Oxford finished in 1845, more than two thousand years later.

Pediment
This is the triangular part of the roof. It often has statues or sculptures in it.

Sculptures
These are often used to make the pediment interesting to look at. The sculptures sometimes tell a story. The ones on the Parthenon are from myths about the gods.

Triglyphs
These are the carvings with three vertical bars. Some Greek buildings used to be made from wood, and some experts think these triglyphs are supposed to look like the end of roofing timbers

Columns
These hold up the pediment and make the building look impressive. There are three types of Greek column.

ALL AROUND US

Spot the column!

Match the picture with the description

Corinthian column
- acanthus leaf ornaments
- complex decoration

Doric column
- oldest design
- plain, simple, no base

Ionic column
- capita (the part at the top) in the shape of ram's horns
- drum-shaped stone base

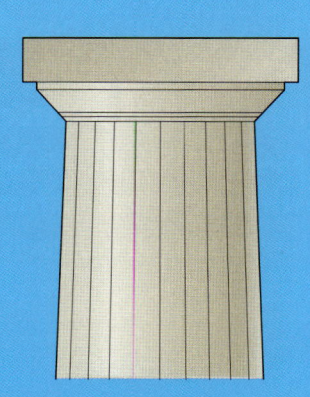

HAVE THE GREEKS GIVEN US MORE THAN ANY OTHER CIVILIZATION?

The way we live now is built upon the ideas, inventions and discoveries of the past. The ideas we use every day have come from many different cultures, from America to the Middle East. However, many scholars and thinkers call Greece 'the cradle of **civilization**' – so is it fair to say that we, in modern Britain, owe more to the Greeks than to anyone else?

In terms of mathematics, we clearly owe much to the Middle East. Our Arabic number system is efficient and simple, and the most significant number of all – the 'place holder' which allows us to manipulate tens and units – is an Arabic word: *zero*. However, the Greeks also gave us a branch of mathematics – *geometry* – and the rules discovered by Greek mathematicians like Euclid, Archimedes and Pythagoras are still used today in architecture, industry and science.

The English language too has come to us from cultures all over the world, particularly Latin, the language of Ancient Rome: many English words have Latin *roots*, *prefixes* or *suffixes*, and our writing system is based on Latin characters. It is fair to say, though, that the Latin language had its roots in Greek, and the alphabetic system that allows us to represent sounds with letters was refined in Greece. Many familiar words are directly taken from the Ancient Greek language.

One such word is *philosophy*, and this is an area in which the Greeks have been particularly influential. They are responsible for many important ideas which underlie the way we think and live, such as 'the Socratic method' of logical analysis. Although our political and legal institutions are often based on Roman models, the key idea underlying the way we are governed is the Greek word *democracy*.

Similarly, the main religion in Britain, Christianity – though based in the Jewish faith which sprang up in the Middle East – was profoundly influenced by the writings of the Greek **philosopher**, Aristotle. The Greeks' tolerant attitude to religion is also an important legacy: they thought, as we do today, that people should have a choice as to what they believe.

The details of our daily lives have clearly been shaped by civilizations far and wide: – paper money from Ancient China, medicines from the Middle East, music based in the traditions of Europe and America. Nevertheless, if one looks at all the evidence – not forgetting **architecture**, sporting events, education and theatre – it seems that, of all civilizations, the greatest legacy of gifts has been from the Greeks.

GLOSSARY

Acropolis the heart of ancient city of Athens, where the Athenians worshipped

alliances friendships made between city states or other groups to support each other

architect a person who designs buildings and spaces

architecture the science of building, planning and design

arms military weapons

armour protective covering for soldiers

besieged surrounded by enemy soldiers for a long time

capsize, capsizing when a boat is turned upside down in the water

city state the area controlled by one Greek city

civilized a way of living which is organized and orderly

democracy a way of governing where everyone has the opportunity to vote for their choice of government

domestic relating to home or local area

elected an elected person is chosen by people to do something, e.g. lead a country

ephorate the council of Spartan governors

Euclid a Greek mathematician

falcatas a sword with a curved blade

flanks edges or sides of an advancing army on the battlefield

gymnasium a school in ancient Athens

legend a story which is based on a true event

lyre a stringed musical instrument

melodrama a play full of dramatic excitement and emotion

military exploits great things done in battle by soldiers

mosaics a picture or pattern made from lots of small tiles

myth a story, usually about gods and goddesses

narrator the person who tells a story

philosopher someone who studies philosophy, which is the science of how to think

politics the activities of a government when leading a country

priestesses a woman who is in charge of religious ceremonies

propaganda information used to promote a point of view, usually political and one-sided

Punic Wars the wars between the ancient Greeks and the Romans

strategy the planning of a battle or a war

stylus a pointed tool for writing on wax tablets

truce an agreement to stop fighting

wax tablets flat sheets of wax, backed with wood, used to write on

BIBLIOGRAPHY

Non-Fiction

Burrell and Connolly, P *Oxford First Ancient History,*
ISBN 0-19-521373-4

Connolly, P *Ancient Greece,*
ISBN 0-19-910764-5

Connolly, P and Dodge, H *The Ancient City,*
ISBN 0-19-521582-6

Connolly, P *The Ancient Greece of Odysseus*
ISBN 0-19-910532-4

Deary, T Groovy *Greeks (Horrible Histories)*
ISBN: 0590132474

Fiertear, P *Theseus and the Minotaur* Web Non-Fiction
ISBN 0-19-917375-3

Langley, A *Alexander the Great,*
ISBN 0-19-910196-5

Peach, S *The Greeks (Illustrated World History),*
ISBN: 0746003420

Pearson, A *Ancient Greece*
ISBN 086318909

The Oxford Children's Encyclopaedia of History,
ISBN 0-19-910776-9

Oxford Children's History of the World ,
ISBN 0-19-910500-6

Fiction

McCaughrean, G *The Odyssey*
ISBN 0-19-274183-7

Picard, B.L. *The Iliad*
ISBN 0-19-275074-7

The Odyssey
ISBN 0-19-275075-5

Internet

www.schoolhistory.co.uk

www.spartacus.schoolnet.co.uk

www.thebritishmuseum.ac.uk/compass

www.bbc.co.uk/history/ancient/greeks/index.shtml

www.angliacampus.com/public/pri/history/greeks/

www.4learning.co.uk/essentials/history/units/
greeks_bi.shtml

www.stcatherines.surrey.sch.uk/greek_pottery_page.html

www.st-dominics-jun.hackney.sch.uk/ancientgreeks/
Pages/GREEK%20homes.html

www.gridclub.com/fact_gadget/the_greeks/
spotlight_on_ancient_greeks/

www.digitalbrain.com/digitalbrain/web/subjects/
1.%20primary/ks2his/su4/mod1/?verb=view

www.highlandschools-virtualib.org.uk/
primary_curriculum/greeks.htm

www.mythweb.com/index.html

Organizations

Ashmolean Museum, Oxford

British Museum, London

The Museum of Classical Archaeology,
University of Cambridge, Cambridge

INDEX

Academy 15
Acropolis 4, 42
Aegean Sea 5–7, 10
Aeschylus 37
agora 19
Alexander the Great 8
alphabet 9, 38
Aphrodite 33
Apollo 33
Apollo Bassae 4
Archimedes 9, 28–31
Archimedes' inventions 28, 29–31
architecture 18–19, 40–41
Ares 33
aristocracy 10
Aristophanes 37
armour 20
Ashmolean 41
Athena 33
Athenian League 7
Athenian life 11–12, 14–15
Athens 7–8, 10–12, 14, 40

barracks (Spartan) 13
Battle of Marathon 8, 22, 24–25
Battle of Salamis 8, 22–23

chiton 16, 17
city states 6, 7–9, 12, 18
clothes 16, 17
columns 40, 41
Corinthian column 41

Demeter 33
democracy 9, 10
diekplous 21

Dionysus 33
Doric column 41

Ephorate 11
Euclid 28
Euripides 37

falacatas 20

Grammatistes 15
Greek gods 18, 32–34
gymnasium 14, 16, 19

Hieron 30
Hera 33
Hercules 32
himation 17
hoplite 20
houses 18

Ionic column 41

Kitharistes 15

language 38–39
levers 31

Mediterranean 5–7
Menelaus 22
Miltiades 24
monarchy 10
moussaka 5

oligarchy 10
Olympic Games 9, 34–35

paedagogus 14
Paidotribes 15
pankration 34
Parthenon 4, 40
Peloponnesian Wars 8

pentathlon 35
peplos 16
Persians 8, 23–25
petasos 17
Philippides 25
philosophers 8, 26–27, 43
Plato 8, 10, 26
plays 36–37
playwrights 36–37
Poseidon 33

Romans 9, 28–29, 42–43

Socrates 8, 26–27, 43
soldiers 13, 20
Sophocles 37
souvlaki 5
Sparta 7, 8, 10–13
Spartan Alliance 7
Spartan life 12–13
sports 15–16, 34–35, 43
stylus 14
Syracuse 6, 28–30

temples 4–5, 18, 40–41
Thales 9
The Trojan War 8, 22
theatre 19, 36–37, 43
Themistocles 23
timocracy 10
trireme 8, 21, 23
tyranny 10

wars 7–9, 22–25
weapons 20, 21

Xerxes 23
Zeus 33